John Yau (signature)

JOHN YAU

MY
HEART
IS THAT
ETERNAL

Rose

Tattoo

BLACK SPARROW PRESS
SANTA ROSA • 2001

MY HEART IS THAT ETERNAL ROSE TATTOO. Copyright ©
2001 by John Yau.

ACKNOWLEDGMENTS

I would like to thank the editors of *Conduit*, *Denver Quarterly*,
First Intensity, and *Untitled*.

"Double-Headed Creature Features" was published by Makeshift
Press in 2001 with artwork by Max Gimblett, conception and exe-
cution by Tobin Hines.

Black Sparrow Press books are printed on acid-free paper.

LIBRARY OF CONGRESS CATALOGING-IN-PUBLICATION DATA

Yau, John, 1950–
   My heart is that eternal rose tattoo / John Yau
     p.   cm.
   ISBN 1-57423-168-5 (paperback)
   ISBN 1-57423-169-3 (cloth trade)
   ISBN 1-57423-170-7 (signed cloth)
    I. Title.

PS3575.A9 M94   2001
813'.54—dc21   2001052818

For the poets of Berkeley and Oakland

Garrett Caples, Jeff Clark, and Andrew Joron

and for the Heroic Trio

Barbara Guest, Robert Kelly, and Philip Lamantia

Table of Contents

I.

II.

III.

IV.

V.

VI.

MY **HEART** IS THAT **ETERNAL**
Rose Tattoo

I

Samarkand Update

(after Clark Ashton Smith)

In one corner of the main waiting room of a vast, five-sided bus depot, which is one of thirteen sharply peaked structures rising above the terrain, that highly disciplined bands of hooded and numbered gnomes erected along the Silk Road last spring, two winged creatures squat comfortably within their voluminous cotton robes. Identical yellow and blue diamond patterns, they are not a design but some kind of signal or beacon.

Three large red moths hover above them. On each wing there appears to be an eye, almond shaped and outlined in fine black dust, which reminds the figure (the reader), who is sitting almost directly opposite the winged creatures (pages of text), of certain nearly forgotten icons.

Huddled at one end of a long wooden bench (or pew), each creature carefully pores over a large oblong octavo, its pages filled with vertical rolls of helical script. Pages reading pages. The beginning of a hall of mirrors into which these figure have entered.

Hexagonal tiles of scorpions and cantelopes. Symmetrical cerulean blue butterfly stain on wall between two onyx inlaid doors leading to overlapping rings of arrival and departure platforms. Arranged on the flanking windowsills, an anonymous tribute; two rows of nine emerald-colored lizards lying on their backs. Between these offerings, mounted on the wall directly behind the winged figures, is a row of black-and-white photographs taken in one of the three documentary styles that briefly delighted the inhabitants of the surrounding villages.

Seven celebrated eunuchs stare at the ball of bright air gathered before their unblinking eyes, the formal pose of their bald heads and wrinkled countenances frozen in the photograph's collective memory of what a locked room crammed with labeled jars preserves for all eternity in the irregularly numbered vaults carved into the granite substrata beneath the palace basement.

Outside the bus depot, one can hear a crow singing, possibly the one that has been genetically altered; it is covered with a cloak of red feathers and punctuated by a long gold beak. It is said that if one listens carefully to his squawking, one hears him sing of a marketplace where presence and absence barter over what's to be exchanged. It is said that he wants to reclaim a body he longer remembers possessing, a body that he believes existed in the cold corridors of his past.

Others claim, however, that to satisfactorily interpret the crow's song is to exile him from this cylindrical forest, its dense calligraphy, and that whatever words one hears in his cawing are the last and first noises you made in your sleep.

Copied from the Margins

A gouged wall or scratched mirror or both. A pool of brocade swallows in imported smoking jackets. This anthracite shatter was supposed to have been excised pages ago, about the time dinosaurs were abducted by cartoonists in tall rubber boots. Pried loose from every book of handkerchief candy.

C opied from the Margin (2)

Candle smoke coagulates on uneven surface of a heavenly cloud, its shifting plumage. We drop the postcard into a box. Later we boarded a cart headed for the airport. A red cart. A red cart with yellow wheels. The kind that turns backwards in the afternoon sun. When it is a plum floating in peach nectar injected with streaks of delicious poison. Who has time to remember all this someone shouted, arms outstretched, neck muscles pulsing to the digital watch surgically embedded in his right eye. And so we waved good-bye to the dogs before they got too juiced.

S *wan*

I drifted through a string of sand-clogged towns, an ejected blue deity. I got plopped on every floor. I toured the shovel factory and kissed a row of obedient mitten warmers. It wasn't enough to satisfy the supplicants, their mouths busy forming the platitudes by which they raised themselves from the nearly alive but not quite dead status. I climbed through the rungs in a zoo. I embraced statues after I gouged out their eyes.

Another Name for It

Called "Furtive Burst of Happiness" by those who were lucky enough to have witnessed only its last coat of effects, the plague traveled leisurely toward the outlying districts, usually in the shape of a well-dressed gentleman accompanied by two highly trained and effective children. No commentary has been added to suggest anything more about them. Distinctly patterned ties, delicate blue ridges shifting beneath taut cold skin. Musculature unlike any other seen in these parts. They are said to have talked about turkeys, but we became them, feathered hulls dotting the rotted landscape.

Almost Between a Rock and a Hard Place

Sable brush poised above what is to be a young's girl's head, its dredged accumulations. Curtsy gaze inserted into muddy paste, its thickening slime. Stares into the future, that blank canvas, where they might one day be waiting, tall in the leaning light. Doesn't see that they've already slipped into the paint behind his shadow, that room he will never turn around and see, that room where hands and mouths find the shapes by which memory patches its tent.

Scenes from Family Life

Sunday evening's ration of moonlight is momentarily stalled on the outskirts of Belchertown. In a suburban train station parking lot, small inexpensive looking cars begin settling into their imported, overnight bags, while the library's marble stairs turn pink and crusty as the day-old frosting of a birthday cake left on the porch of an empty house. Across the street, paper clouds submit their whispers to the empty bookshelves. Yes, about now a winding row of half-clothed figures is quietly vanishing into a tablecloth of manicured tree trunks. No one is going back to the windows to touch the dust. We will miss out on dessert if we do.

After reading the latest pornographic installment he received in the mail, Mr. Porcupine goes to the refrigerator and gets a boatload secreted in his quills. Even as the remaining minutes deposit their feverish fleas on appropriate recipients, the following portrait begins to take the place of the subject, who was once a dandy and even handsome in his day. My paws, Pablo croons, all waxy and percussive, are beginning to grip the stars dissolving in the delirium of tomorrow's wet announcements.

So began the trend of blue leather gloves and white linen tuxedoes. So began an era dominated by hordes of wandering book clubs

While Waiting for the Weather to Retreat

Cirrus debris tans the fluorescent cup-
boards, its stacks of broken beads and
branded hags. Quick scan registers further evidence
of former inhabitants' habits. Broken venetian blinds,
their slats spread open like the ribs of an antique fan
or prehistoric bird, the papery skin torn off. Words
written on cheap papyrus strip: We can't go back,
either in time or place. Besides, it's cold beneath the
bridge, its bubbles trapped between bricks. How to
surface in this world where all surfaces recede?

A shadowy city-like city ransacks the dreams rusting
on the floor beside us. Under a ceiling crowded with
blue seraphim resting on lizard wings, their tails cir-
cling one of the many moons that adorn this eye
peering in at those still lying in their beds, tousled
hair and entangled limbs. Ankle bracelets and hiero-
glyph tattoos. One of the seraphim, Miss Anaconda

Erotic Asphyxiation, is about to slither a message through one of the few cubes of space still ruled by time's nameless elves.

In another part of town, the part near the burning bus station, a lanky shadow in a second-hand camel hair coat reminds his ovoid companion, all cerulean and cogged, that telekinetic sandstorms, parasite transmitters, and acts of unnecessary vigilance are among the many categories whose charts they have yet to graph. Molten lead spreads its map slowly across the gum-infested floor. Secretion stains on far wall, below signed, limited edition posters of celebrated eunuchs.

"Come, let us bathe in a bucket of warm tears."

"Yes, my sweet cockerel, let us sip foam with the lips we obtained from the previous connoisseurs of flight."

This is how the first morning of our trip began. Muslin clouds already folded and stacked on upper shelves. Another part of us continues to float off. Meanwhile, a band of gnomes, their shriveled fruit cramped in pith helmets, capsizes in the far corner of a semi-reliable lake a painter is trying to render into pigments, his mitten face askew.

An oblong slab illuminates what's behind the rest of this story, a nearly true story because no one has ever survived to tell it.

The *Perfectionist*

He realized that he would never find the right color, size, or material. The light had a crooked slant to it, crackling murmurs in its poured gold. In the morning the dust was too thick, too heavy, just there. Between him and there, it's it.

S*horter Version*

C arved from a tree.

Threaded into the rain.

Becomes a boat book bulk of lightning coat with buttons bon-bons booming inside he rolls until lying face pressed to a dirty window called sky or a sky called heaven on wheels.

The end of all stories is the story he keeps telling himself and the fish.

Who was there when the final views arrived?

O pening
Scene

One night, he left his studio without unhooking the phone. A row of mottled artifacts took its place on the shelf. His wife glided inside the hut and sat above the fire. The steam was starting to stew. She had better things to squeeze.

The sound of a baby's rattle in a thunderstorm.

Robert Walser Speaks about Robert Walser

Each snowflake is bigger than a doll's mitten. I know, I was a doll once. A cloth body stuffed with old almanacs, their incorrect forecasts of rain and murder. And like all the dolls before me, I was made to sit on a crowded shelf next to a little girl who had been ordered to sit still and who never moved again. She is not my sister I told them before they closed the door, but none of them listened to the silence they left behind.

It is not supposed to be winter yet. It isn't even supposed to be spring or summer. And fall has yet to fall from the trees. So why is the faux-marble sky the top of a seesawing ocean. And why am I adrift along the bottom, a semi-retired fish waiting to be memorialized by slime. Is it time to change? Time to hang up one life and to wear another until it too is worn out? A bandaged coat, a charred shoe. Are these the exchanges one makes when waiting for the seasons to appear, however briefly?

After I secrete my monogrammed diapers in the glove compartment, I slip into the lush crevices of my giraffe suit. This is the house where the shadows of inaccuracy are squeezed into moths made of egg whites.

I never thought growing up was going to be so bumpy and crusty. So full of dried milk. So full of tears sprouting from a face I haven't gotten used to wearing, having just arrived. But the really big questions just seem to be getting bigger. These days they take up the entire newspaper, even the sports page and ads for corrective surgery.

Don't we all need a little gentle correcting here and there? a maroon Hawaiian shirt to convince us we are thinner, and even make us feel a little less marooned, on the flight from Bombay, Ohio to Lachrymae, Wisconsin? Must we always approach a mirror from the side?

Who shall I talk about if not the one others confuse with me?

Have you ever wondered why names are like bicycles? And why you never forget how to ride them down the hallways of institutions, especially when they are on fire and everyone is sleepwalking toward the newly renovated auditorium?

I like to sit near the back, under the false constellations. The room doesn't grow darker. In fact, it doesn't grow at all. And neither do we.

It's cold out here beneath the night sky, its face riddled with lice. To keep warm, I talk back to the shadows without trying to plumb anything more about their relationship between gesture and language; they remain as black and impenetrable as my dead father's heart.

II

U*ntiled 1*

Eyes implanted in bulging wings won't guide us this time. Nor eyes painted on sharp prows.

U*ntiled II*

A*lpha, Edison, and Omega*, a mecha-nized voice begins emptying its bottle over the latest display case of artificial clouds. Pink and orange pulsing from within, lavender and purple in the creases. No beeps or blips, honks or chomps interfere with its syllabic production.

Has the audience finally learned that the old trails include this reassuring cul-de-sac? Long tunnels down which your legs churn, buttery columns melting into the stone latticework, rats chasing your charitable implants.

Warning: If not properly and immediately cultivated, any hairless protuberance you encounter might one day prove catastrophic.

And now that this warning has been delivered in a variety of languages, signs, and easy-to-understand formulas, we (a swarm of terrestial homunculi) are exercising the right to withdraw our non-stick mandibles.

U ntiled III

(*A False Painting*)

They are hunters on their way home, as if hunting is the sole reason they gather before dawn, and begin warming their hands with the remains of their oily breath.

Towards evening, with quarried shadows collecting around their imported electric fire, its iron logs, they hunker down and wait for their harnesses to be loosened.

Neatly and efficiently imbedded in a crease of realistic shadows, the youngest one remembers the flesh prints he saw the night before, on a staircase descending from the honeycomb of a watery moon.

Untiled IV

In back of moss hewn pumphouse long rug of once thriving hulk lies beneath plaid salt and dotted brim. A sideburn pilot and his headless copper stamp. Scooped out, dubbed into hollow. Leafy pan all wet with greased stones. Sallow disc or munched moon. The lurching bag and shoulder rack hanging from an exquisitely rendered branch, veronese green in the yellow lamp of igneous moonlight.

U*ntiled V*

(*Unsent Postcard*)

We have been lying here since the first cloud was posted above the prairie. Another part of us floats off the overgrown page, while the rest rises from the embers glowing in the flooded folds of our drifting.

Untiled VI

(*In Place of a Dream*)

We swallowed the silhouette powder and went smooth near the lingerie. Red windows in small jars. Stacks of books waiting to be hoisted toward the sky's smoke. Somnambulist pharoah with carved black eyebrows and full length pout. Club toting satyrs roaming the streets he has had erected beside numbered scenes of locked grass. Winter's plumage, we hear ourselves say, will never be different.

U *ntiled VII*

The dream needed to be repeated once, at least the memory of it, to an audience of educated grasshoppers. Otherwise the spell would be broken, and their wishes would turn into a spoonful of rust stuck in the mouths of recently disfigured statues.

A man and a woman, their loyalties expected to be expended on others. Once the emperor learned of their alliance, he buried them alive. Facing in different directions, interred in separate urns, in secret locations in distant villages. The emperor didn't get what he wanted. For one of them didn't regret relinquishing the flesh, while the other looked forward to becoming a bodiless being, a spirit. They didn't get what they wanted either, but then many eons later perhaps they did.

They met in a museum beside the dead emperor's chariot, its teams of terracotta horses. They vowed that they would bury their newest life and begin again. They were going to burn the emperor's chariot and free the horses from the hardened earth packed around their sinews and flesh. They would become bodiless beings by releasing themselves (and the horses) from their material manifestations, their beauty.

In the morning, you took the commuter train north, toward the brick house perched on a manicured hill, a soft monument, while I walked south, toward the elevator that requires a plastic key.

Last night, you woke up and said, it isn't a dream. That's the way I remembered it happening.

U*ntiled* *VIII*

(*Movie Plots #13 through 39*)

He was an overweight deodorant sales-man who lacked certain essential props: a pedestal on which to display his carefully cropped photographs of various fossils, forgeries, and fusions; a neatly pressed charcoal gray suit, complete with handmade cotton shirt and handpainted silk tie depicting a fleet of triumphant triremes entering an otherwise silent harbor, its lighthouse a woman's arm carved into smoke; a customized bronze frame for his advanced degree in the science of odor detection. Meanwhile, she has only just recently managed to flee a cluster of bricks, the severity of their diagonal lines.

They are headed in opposite directions, toward different shores, each promising different shoes, when they collide outside a burning deli, on a corner near a shadowy doorway, its unusual arch, beneath a slant of indecipherable graffiti, beside their towering shadows. After many hours of non-linear communication, perhaps it actually takes eons in another frame of time-space relationships, they—shouldn't we at this point skip their names?—decide to investigate the various dimensions they are convinced an earlier generation has interred on the outskirts of the igloo mall, its cobblestone walkways lined with empty cradles.

Walking, one hoof in front of the other.

In the distance, a sleek silvery bus crammed with winged passengers.

U*ntiled IX*

(Posted Postcard)

Mountain night embraces its shadows in an otherwise empty courtyard, until all the stars are mounted on pikes. Rapture in bandage profile.

U _ntiled X_

(*False Painting #2*)

Report of body stolen from laundry closet of Motel Sumeria #7356, which is one of the outer sod units, all its primary colors framed in mud. In the distance, a statuary filtration facility clogged with animal hair.

Detail of fingerprints hardening on ledge of wax roof.

Rhyming hills, tremulous apertures.

Whose pen is overwhelming this cancelled village with tilting slashes?

Untiled XI

(*After Franz von Stuck and Arnold Bocklin*)

The clouds's black ropes stretch across a candle stunned lake. Pools of light thinned to this world's lost interior, its faceted shadows. We cannot enter this room without bringing the floor on which we are standing. A window hovers before us, on wings a man once held in his hands, each feather soaked in the colors he extracted from the bones of his ancestors.

U*ntiled* XII

Tubes of Egyptian paint and pails of Edison mud. Did you see where I put the seismograph or what happened to the soothsayer's lake of things? Our manager is a horse. No, he neither sings nor dances. Wouldn't that be a little too much for you big city dictionaries to believe?

U*ntiled* *XIII*

(*First Variation on XII*)

The Cimmerian entourage is packing their jade flutes, aluminum plows, and iron aprons. Their tubes of Babylonian blue and Chinese yellow. The big one likes to squeeze the little one's inner chamber, rub the music emanating from the ivory tub. I'm sure something got lost in the translation, maybe a clutch of hair, the ceremonial wig some believe endows the wearer with magical powers. Or the ibogene the tunic clad official waves above his tiny elegant head, the one the government returned to him after he failed his first examination.

U*ntiled* XIV

The deluge is approaching the mermaid station. Too bad about the little travelers. We'll not be seeing too many more like them anytime soon.

U ntiled XV

(After an Unknown Artist)

Sparks rise and lodge inside timbers of rotting sky. Capsized clouds. Who among us now walks along world's lower ledges, where bonfires lick the winged shadows? Who enters and emerges from the huts posted at the edge of night's domain? Who are these creatures who have taken it upon themselves to copy down the inscriptions left in the Book of Air?

Untitled XVI

Forests advance and recede throughout the accounts that have come down to us, calligraphic coils some have speculated are carnivores (or disgruntled poets) winding tightly around the stately process of narrative that always seems to be moving toward the furnace sun.

And always, towards morning, after the stars are carefully removed, and the remaining streaks are replaced by scalloped gusts of air, there appears a row of holes through which the day's first rain begins to drip.

U*ntiled* *XVII*

The rain conductor glosses the crickets, their long shiny legs trembling in the waterglass morning.

U*ntiled* _XVIII_

(*Guide to Museum Collection*)

Woman with Child and Anteater

Man Handing Woman Bigger Stick of Gum

Still-Life with Contents of Bankrupt Neighbor's Garage

Newly Married Couple Posing before Shiny Shovel

Man Bent Over Wristwatch of Dead Boss

Landscape with Two Swarms of Flies

Italian Landscape with View of Glistening Firehouse

Interior with Young Man Standing on Window Ledge

Ship Off Coast with Large Gust of Pollution

Interior with Striped Dog and Leftovers

Market in Dutch Town with Phony Eskimo

*Portrait of an Unreliable Witness Surrounded by
    Angels*

Mud-Colored Faces of the False Penitents

*Landscape with Overturned Barge and Drowning Ice
    Skaters*

Still Life with Severed Hand and Forged Painting

U*ntitled* *XIX*

(*Recent Acquisitions*)

*Man on Horse Assailing Rebels with Machine Gun
and Rocket Launcher*

*The Emperor Seated in Front of His Tent, Listening to
the Stars*

Dog Defecating on Emperor's Lacquered Dinner Plate

The Princess and Her Playthings, The Smiths

*The President with His Favorite Recipe for Spotted
Snake*

The Palace of the Newly-Calmed Sea

*Welcoming the Arrival of Spring with a Golden
Hammer*

III

The Last Emperor Lives on the Moon

"The chair of poetry is empty."
Frank O'Hara

It first occurred to him shortly after he finished sighing audibly for the audience gathered in the First Hall of Ancestors. Although no one in the audience, which was as still and attentive as a reflecting pool, was apt to reach the same conclusion just yet, that would take more time and parcels of evidence, the emperor realized that the *now* they inhabited was different from the *then*, however recent, in that it, the all consuming it, was no longer a possibility, but rather an inevitable likelihood. Time's passage, he realized, had undergone a fundamental change. And soon he would no longer be what he once was, an infallible being, but would instead be just a long-winded footnote to his former existence.

Possessing a philosophical disposition, the emperor equated it with death-in-life, rather than life and death or life-in-death. Such a death, which is to say life, was what would soon embrace him, as he would, more than likely, gladly embrace it, having no other choice if he wished to continue enjoying the mortal part of his existence, the immortal part having become both a foregone conclusion before he was born and a part of world that was about to cease its existence. And because death-in-life was his future, life in death receded into the *then*, like a custom or holiday that was no longer observed. Instead, this *now* stretched beyond itself; it threatened to become both perfect and permanent, a purgatory from which one never left.

His attenuated sigh was a signal to the audience, they could now begin readying themselves to leave the hall in which they had been sitting all morning, bowing and scraping on cue, as they listened enthusiastically to the reading of the official edicts concerning the rules governing night baseball games, acceptable names of villages and their bowling teams, and progress reports on the construction of seven and eight lane highways in remote and farflung provinces.

Knowing that he had not truly perfected the aching arc of his sigh as he had been shown by his teachers, the emperor was startled to realize that it could still be of use to him in his next life, and that he should continue practicing meshing together its soft unfolding with a barely noticeable bodily shudder. After all, he was both the emperor and the leading actor of his time, both the figure appointed by heaven and the one who enabled others to glimpse heaven's existence.

It was the next life that he would inhabit that suddenly concerned the emperor. He realized that the designation he was about to receive would never be corrected, that it would, in fact, never be shifted from its position of finality, and that in all likelihood he would be buried forever beneath the distribution of this epithet in the annals and annuals, bios and biopics, calendars and cylinders about to be loosed upon the world.

And with each tall tell-all tale following one after the other, like ants scurrying toward sugar, and the accompanying embellishments and elaborations growing increasingly more fulsome, there was nothing the emperor could do. He was the Last Emperor, the final one to ascend to his kingdom's immense lacquered throne. He was the end of a mystery that would never be unraveled. He had been put away before he was ready to be consigned to a niche. His life was a jar that would never be opened, its scents and flavors and suble accents would never hold another individual's attention, would never induce states of rapture and moments of helpless envy bordering on the worshipful.

He briefly considered his options, knowing there were less than few. Protest was, of course, out of the question. Emperors, even those who are not the last, but are known as such, never protest. It's unseemly. They prefer to silently lobby the stars, to try and have heaven intercede on their behalf. After all, they are heaven's spokesman and medium.

Acting would now play a different role in this emperor's life.

He knew the following scenario was inevitable. A banner headline floats above a round, regal countenance imbued with unknowable thoughts: *The Last Days of the Last Emperor*. The well-known author describes what the emperor ate as the end drew near, what he watched on television, and what kinds of music he listened to, as he stared out the window of his palace. There is no mention of the baths, concubines or sex. The emperor was solemn until the end; he did not frolic. As far as the public knows, or cares to know, the Last Emperor most likely died a virgin. He could not have been both happy and oblivious right up until his untimely end. Such a scenario is unacceptable to a world committed to realism. The well-known writer earned his reputation because of his belief in realism; it was why he was highly rewarded. He knew he was being paid handsomely to gratify the inchoate hunger of his reading public. The Last Emperor could not have been happy right up until the end. The Last Emperor could not have believed that he would rise straight to heaven when the end drew nigh.

Over time the grainy screen of this dignified silhouette will grow less distinct, like a snowman on a sunny day. But the words declaring the end of the story will continue flying into the future, carrying its irrefutable assertion. Eventually, a verbal equivalent will be inserted into the once physically occupied space. An unsubstantiated description of a puny man perched uncomfortably atop the thick, presumably velvet pleats of an oversized relaxing chair is entered into the collective image bank of free associations.

The chair, we will learn, is a typical gift from a foreign dignitary who has come and paid respects to this hapless mediator between heaven and earth. It is a two-sided gift, as the chair is always too large to be comfortable and thus a physically obvious rebuke of the emperor's connection to heaven. That's one argument, the other being that in his presently constituted form, nothing should fit the emperor perfectly.

So the large chairs are seen by some as the right size, the only size, befitting an emperor.

Few know, however, that the bedeviled figure in the newspaper, and the one that waits blankly to be greeted by bland foreign dignitaries accompanied by large empty chairs, aren't even the same person. Both are doubles, stand-ins for the real emperor, who prefers to stand off to the side and is said to pretend to be someone else, usually a minor official of no real importance, a figurehead. As someone who goes unnoticed, he can record the various reactions, official and unofficial. He records his own life as if it belonged to someone else, which, if one thinks about it, it does. The question is "who does it belong to?"

This is where the story gets tangled and untangled. And here. And here. And, of course, here.

Where is heaven? How might someone like myself, a humble and honest cobbler, get there? These are the kinds of annoying questions that greet every emperor, whether he is the mayor of a large island city or the king of a small landlocked country full of casinos. It is when the unspoken becomes frequently spoken, and a nearly inaudible murmur grows into a vast inescapable chorus, that emperors should begin considering their alternatives.

> What do I have to do to gain access to my
> retirement fund?
> Do I remember all the codes, passwords,
> and handshakes?
> Can I reach those suitcases my
> predecessors stashed away just in case the
> inevitable came to pass during their reign?
> Where are the deeds to the real estate I
> own abroad?
> What countries accept ex-emperors
> without prying into their past?
> How might I continue being an emperor
> in name only?

Rent a Highness was started by a former emperor known for his movie star good looks and olympic physique. Scrupulous about the code of behavior that ex-emperors should follow, this one refused all roles Hollywood offered him. There is only one role I can play, and it's not a role and I am not playing it. As the offers began piling higher and higher, he called a press conference and announced that the reality of being an ex-emperor was, on every conceivable level, far more satisfying than any fantasy Hollywood could cook up for him. Hollywood's vast kingdoms and limitless empires were far less satisfying than the small landlocked one he ruled, however briefly. His memories of his life as emperor were enough to sustain him for eternity.

This only made the offers increase, and the ex-emperor was soon forced to go into hiding near the island of Capris. It is during this period that he authored the highly touted *Code of Behavior for Ex-Emperors*. He was the first peacefully deposed ruler— one who in fact willingly surrendered his throne—to suggest that ex-emperors should not consort with ex-dictators. They were to exist on a higher plane of possibility, however diminished it had become.

He made one exception, which is that he allowed that ex-emperors could and should be polite to ex-dictators at large, well-attended poetry readings, as such gatherings were likely to lure all kinds of pretenders to poetry's throne, as well as compel dictators of one sort or another to make an appearance. Within this setting an ex-emperor would gain in stature by being visibly cordial to all who came his way.

The Last Emperor knew he wasn't the final manifestation of that physical body, that there were others who would gladly take his place. He wasn't even the next to the last minor deity to be swaddled in this epithet. He was, in fact, one of many emperors (and their legions of doubles) who have had to disguise themselves in order to escape one of many nearly identical villages and towns dotting the landscape, their barns and arcades engulfed in flames.

The emperor heard about the others, the pretenders who didn't get rid of their costumes in time. A few stories circulated by the anonymous tipsters that pursue the details of each emperor's death, like a dog chasing its tail.

In addition to the hundreds of doubles and stand-ins, each sworn to secrecy, the Last Emperor is rumored to have had at least eleven half-brothers and twenty-two distant cousins, and that their resemblance to each other is believed to have passed the most demanding tests and examinations devised by the Emperor's network of assassins and secret police. However, the exact number of look-alikes remains in dispute because the counting system used in this particular's Emperor's court had not yet been refined to the point that the set could include fractions.

Among the various heirs who can rightfully claim to be the Last Emperor, this Emperor's exact place in the numerical sequence that the earliest round of sages predicted would stretch to infinity is a matter of personal concern. If he is not the last or even the next to the last, then what is he? Is he simply a number? Or is he something more than a number? Is he a number whose meaning increases with each passing season?

If all the Last Emperors could complain, who would stop and listen to them? The members of the Bureau of Denunciation? Who would they denounce? The god-makers? The deification process, it seems, has been undergoing a change.

Many sightings have been reported since one of the Last Emperors (or was it one of the pretenders to the throne?) was photographed jogging across a sunlit dappled parking lot during the middle of hunting season. In one of the more intriguing versions posted on the web it is said that he is gripping two green duffel bags stuffed with uncollected refunds. In the background of another document one sees the ominous blue shape of a shadow cast by a maroon cassock draped over a velvety black caisson.

This version of the last Emperor was not radically different from those who preceded him. He was acceptably small when he was supposed to be small; and he grew in accordance with the ancient chart's predictions.

Each of the Last Emperors was more ordinary than his audience had come to expect. He possessed neither distinguishing facial tics nor celebrity markers. He mindlessly sifted through a neighbor's mail. He was a middle son who made a brief appearance in the waning moments of a six-hour television special: *Mysteries of the Middle Kingdom.* You have to look carefully to spot him sitting atop a marble tortoise in the winter palace playground. One of his cousins is viciously kicking a headless statue of an unidentified deity. Another is playing quietly in the yellow dirt. And still another is seen shouting at something or someone unseen.

In the only known photograph of what many believe to be the true Last Emperor, the eldest of the grand viziers stands nearby, pointing a long carved ribbon of a stick at a fleet of clouds stalled overhead. Many leading authorities have speculated upon the nature of the lesson the young Emperor is supposed to be absorbing at that moment, but so far none of the explanations have proved convincing. If you should like to enter the contest, which will end in less than ninety-nine days, please send your entry and entry fee to the following address: *Albert's Charitable Chariot Service, Winter Palace Highway, Upper North Fork of the Middle Kingdom.*

In the other, now much disputed photograph, a thin shadow is surrounded by a large squadron of gun toting, turbaned eunuchs. It is drizzling and gray, and the solemn entourage is gathered on a turn-of-the century train station's black granite platform. A curl of graphite smoke rises in the distance. Dozens of smiling blue grackles are gathered in the iron lattices overhead. Beneath the plume of smoke a train. And within the train someone of great importance, but not royalty, is sitting alone in the dining car, surrounded by monogrammed plates piled high with exotic smoked meats and wind-cured fruits.

In the next coach, which is unmonogrammed but well-appointed, three of the five remaining waiters gamble their month's wages and winnings, while the other two now penniless waiters consider which method of suicide would prove the least painful and most efficient. Two extremely large red ants crawl across the titanium white wainscotting. Finally, one penniless figure looks at the other and asks what will prove to be a fateful question for all involved: "Would you consider making just one more bet before we depart this world?"

Like others in the row stretching out on either side of him, the Last Emperor received a special or "endowed" number and a silk robe embroidered with the appropriate pairs of animals, celestial signs, and good luck seals from the outer provinces. Following the prevailing customs of the day, the Emperor's team of bathing attendants and night nurses periodically consulted three astrologers, four holy divinators, and five operators on the psychic hotline, with all their suggestions entered into a floating data bank.

Even at a young age, the Emperor considers his life to be the residue of other lives, which disturbs many of the elderly villagers, particularly those who wish to live near a brand new, dried fish outlet and a mall full of wooden carts crammed with bushels of fresh vegetables.

One of the the last of the Last Emperors likes to watch television game shows. He drinks tall glasses of cold tea and eats large bags of fortune cookies. He has them delivered by a wholesale discount store on lower Broadway, near the burnt-out shell of City Hall. On the weekends he watches semi-pro wrestling and amateur dog sled racing on one of the lesser known sports channels. During the week, he works on his doctoral thesis regarding the migration of emperors without kingdoms. His advisor has warned him not to make his thesis into a novel, that the university is interested only in facts and opinions. When discussing the Last Emperor, it seems that fiction and fantasy have at best a small but dubious place of honor. One must be a footnote to a fact, he told himself, gathering immense comfort from his understanding of what his professor told him.

It was at this moment that he realized he was both a poet and emperor.

IV

C*adium Deposits, Cobalt Traces, and Ocher Mist*

Consider the anonymous artist whose only known surviving work is the small, waterstained canvas, *Still-Life with Ghost of Angry Ancestor.* A faded woman in a short green fur coat and pointed red rubber slippers is laughing at a black and yellow fire hydrant. Here, I would like to propose that the latter detail suggests that the painter was familiar with the seaside town of Bumblebee Flats.

A folding moon is unceremoniously draped above two shepherds, both cloaked in nearly identical flannel. One is skinny, the other pregnant. They are not to be confused with the ovals looking at them. Often they stare back, like defiant squirrels, but their feathers are dull and the scene is beginning to be crowded with traces of snow. Over the years more shadows have slipped into the grooves behind them, while in both of the flanking panels the houses on the cliffs continue to burst with comfortable flames.

Gray clouds lick the soot embedded in the canvas's frayed weave.

The titular head of the city council mentions that the painting that most people wish could be returned to its owner is: *Dog Defecating on the Emperor's Lacquered Dinner Plate*. This seems the obvious choice. But, after a short fireworks of debate, his rival proposes another possibility; *The Emperor Seated in Front of His Tent, Listening to the Stars*.

Waltz of lug and drag. Three ogres argue over a baloney sandwich.

The rabbit stops and the doe raises her head. Had they heard the first pebbles trickling down the slope? Or was it the sound of the morning train colliding with the rain the sculptor has left behind? He told his beleaguered young assistant, all stout grasp, that he would rather join a pilgrimage to a convention of pancake smugglers than wait for another panorama to construct its place on the thunderstorm's mottled shelf.

The man behind us is warning his friends, none of whom are visible. We are glad not to be among them, but here in the fluted gusts of winter diminishing to a glittering trickle. Hints of a song tremble in your hair, its short black sheen.

In a far off city, a fleet of mechanical dogs raises their wooden paws in unison. Their leader has done something unexpected and laid a golden egg.

H eraclitus's Parking Lot

The retired encyclopedist decides to retreat to his rented bungalow, which overlooks a dried-up lake, its cracked muddy crater filled with rusted objects from an earlier era in history's torrential downpour. He fondles his woodpecker skull. A loaf of honeysuckle bread sits on the kitchen counter, surrounded by squadrons of ruby-colored flies. The holding pattern they have endorsed looks familiar, but the retired encyclopedist can't quite figure out why.

Do you believe that the fringe elements have started making themselves known to those hunkered down near what they believe is the center? Is that why the local newspaper blossoms into flames right after we put it down, the words curling into smoke? The eggs are cold again, the toast soggy, the butter melted. Are we to remind ourselves that these are signs of time's advance scouts? Or is the aging process obvious to the clocks mounted inside stones?

For reasons no one can satisfactorily explain, the workmen stopped building the highway once it reached the edge of an afternoon's tesselated shadow cast by the border of the next county. Such breathtaking precision is the result of something more than just a secret mandate.

I own the lot where the tourists park their rented carriages, the carefully tended hill they purposefully stride up, the customized platform on which they stand and point. It is I who framed and shaped this landscape and all the shadows therein. I who am plump but not a god. Nor, however, am I as rich as you might think. For plumpness, however desired or desirable, isn't always a sign of satisfaction, sometimes it is a message from the interior, the frozen screams of dead miners clinging to the prehistoric dust motes preserved in ice. Why I am an ostrich plume in someone else's helmet is the source of much conjecture. The gossip is often troubling, so I have started telling my neighbors it's a riddle made of rat meat and possum innards.

An abandoned swimming pool, its turquoise walls cracked and peeling. A boy's black bathing suit crammed into the mouth of a stuffed bear. Why are you intent on obscuring the rest of my holidays? Are you becoming increasingly virulent about what's left of your sanity? Don't worry, I'm not rushing out the back door, as I know the meadow is full of speckled snakes. However, if I am to lose something of little value, it might as well be my mind. Well, it never did do you much good on days like this, did it? All rainy and thick with cottonball gruel. Why you fatuous ingrate, tubes of foetid miasma are far too good to waste on someone like you, someone born with a burr in his saddle. Want to hear my fondest wish? May tomorrow's merry yellow moon piss on you and your disgruntled loved ones.

True, I didn't always live in an attic overrun with drunken mice. My hair wasn't always clinging perilously to the steep sides of my head. These details were sewn into the fur-lined pockets of an unauthorized edition, which was immensely popular among the inhabitants of the dreary lowlands. Do you hear me, Mister Irving Shakespeare? No story is ever told the same way twice.

Do you see the balloon floating above my noggin, the dotted line connecting me to it? An evil prince has absconded with the walled city I drew there, its many small cubicles laden with expensive knicknacks I managed to retrieve from various purses and shelves, precious little things I hid in my pockets as I made my way through milling crowds. My fellow citizens didn't always understand that I saw things differently. Sure, I was out of sorts. I was out of socks too, but still I managed to join in, and stomp on the poisonous beetles with my stolen parasol and borrowed sandals.

F ilm Adaptations of Five of America's Most Beloved Poems

I t burns and winds. For as long as I can remember, my Sunday task has been to polish the antique wooden perambulator until it gleams like an aluminum breadbox. Do you mind being the landlady's favorite pet? No, Little Igor, raunchy ruminator and muralist to mid-sized manufacturers, these are not the horoscope dials you should be consulting. Look at the fuzzy ones over there, on the pink control panel mounted beneath the custom aquarium populated with poisonous snakes, addled alligators, and small but hearty fish. Have you ever seen such a diverse array of live entertaintment clouding the waters before?

On misty days the sun hangs pale blue over a black diamond sea. Academic painters of every persuasion rise from their imported beach chairs and press their ointment-covered noses against the unnecessarily spotted glass, unaware that cross-eyed snakes are staring back at them. Intrepid mountaineers follow the whistle of the marmot up to the highest crags, and over playgrounds and puddles alike rises the cry of a wounded sea otter, a shiny yodeler fondling the most delectable portion of his imported fish dinner. Meanwhile, a caravan of carrion has been dragged across the sand.

It turns and whines. All motels are penetrated by two sounds—a scream and a complaint. Today, as long ago, these are the two sacred messengers of the Western Nile Plumber's Union and their far flung subsidiary units, Mod and Plod.

Trying to overcome the image of being nothing more than a bunch of loud talking, gum chewing cronies, the union leaders decided to dispense with opening ceremonies and closing sermons. Later, concerned with the rank-and-file's growing resentment of enforced civic duty, some of the leaders voted to reenact well-known gaffes at previous company picnics, while others elected to learn the intricacies of miniature collie and poodle grooming as an alternative to hosting the Sunday car wash. Their favorite costumes included a red satin tuxedo, a cowboy moustache, and nicotine-stained talons. Last month, the duly elected Vice-Secretary issued the following decree: No velvet cones with tassels are allowed to cross the threshold.

High above the Wabash River, its riverbanks lined with quaint cobblestone streets and newly renovated factories, complete with working fire hydrants and helmeted dwarfs scattered discretely among the hordes of wayward children, a foreign possibly alien power has managed to thrust the city's entire work force into a state of suspended animation. The mayor fears the immense stone bridge that was to become a major tourist attraction in the tri-county area will remain unfinished. The pianist is trying to imitate the sound of an oncoming train. No one dreams that the images are stolen from a semi-retired sorcerer while he is dreaming of a minaturized sorcerer who is assassinated and buried in a jelly jar by a quartet of indignant barbers. A hexagonal shield gleams in the ruby-colored gloom descending from the sky. Great ospreys nest in the crowns of the unfinished arches. Four goats wander across the ice. The head goat, William of Upper Broadway, keeps reminding Thutmoss of the likelihood that strange plants are migrating rapidly across the ocean floor.

A man pleads with the creature locked inside the hair dryer to reconsider the wording of their oath. The less said about the source of this rumor, the better. After taking refuge in a deserted gas station containing seven slim coffins, one for each gambling centipede, the highbrow hero—he has a forehead the size of Rhode Island—decides to return from hell to find out why his latest girlfriend didn't follow him to the very ends of the earth. Meanwhile, in a drugstore in Angela, Ohio, an attractive young woman by the name of Akron decides to buy two lottery tickets, one for each side of the coin.

Genghis Chan, the Film

(for Barbara Guest and *The Confetti Trees*)

We parked beyond the black canopy of rain, beneath the dripping trees. It was nearly spring and the full moon was lost behind the red crayon sky.

We sparked the catastrophe that followed us across the blackened plains. Eventually there weren't enough survivors to follow us out of the municipal parking lot.

We stood motionless beneath the dripping trees, across from the shadows embracing beneath a black canopy. The bookstore's specialty was arson and hanging gardens.

Three points of view, but only one story.
Three stories, but only one point of view.

There were three of us, though only one of us was visible to the audience which had gathered in cushioned rows. Blue cushions, yellow rows, green numbers. The story is about a detective, and I could be him. And the story. Or I could be neither. This is why the audience of detectives has paid to see the film, they are gathering clues.

The detectives' favorite game is to disguise themselves as a household appliance. Today they are vacuum cleaners sucking up any flotsam still clinging to the clouds the painter has left behind. The clouds are a red herring, and they are mackerel colored. That is what the painter said before he climbed down from the ladder made of aluminum and other semi-precious metals. He claimed he had never seen a mackerel cloud until he was told to make them look as real and solid as the ones suspended outside.

He looked and saw a spotless black sky, which he remembered as red crayon.

Was it his inner confusion that he was recording? Or had he heard his dead partner Confucius Johnson tell him that the window was still open, but that the sky was no longer there.

L*ake Country*

In winter, we like to walk around the old miser's tidy little lake, and see if we can discover if anything new is amiss. The shadow of a roof sagging beneath the weight of yesterday's insults. An overturned haywagon, its front wheels still spinning. An unfamiliar name added to an already crowded gravestone. The inchoate scribble that interrupts, these are our moments of pleasure.

We know how much these flurries of imbalance annoy the old miser, and, admittedly, we take lip-smacking delight in describing the various new disturbances we have found in the fabric of our everyday life, knowing that after we have left him standing in the fading foyer of his mansion, a rash will suddenly appear and gnaw at him for days, even weeks and possibly months. We like knowing that imaginary vermin have pierced his inherited veneer.

At dawn, after consulting our patented checklist and

pasting on all the necessary attachments, we set out on our fact finding mission, our snowshoes still glistening from last night's moon. In the distance, little dollops of smoke are being ladled into the sky.

Just before noon thrusts its store-bought arrow into the woodpile, we pass a convocation of birds that has gathered beneath a row of stationary shadows to practice some of their more forgettable tunes in an attempt to reach those they one day will be known by. The hours and minutes pass slowly, as they always do in winter when honey thickens in the jar.

When we reach the hermit's hut, we leave the path and walk down to where the cotton-coated crust surrenders to the transparent marble. Peering into the ice, its history of small and lost perfections, we notice a few clouds left over from seasons past. A band of small children waving good-bye to red curtains. A piss-colored dog which has finally managed to catch its tail.

The shadow of a yew tree beside a helmeted man holding an immense mallet.

"Was this how mankind was able to invent the wheel?" you ask. But, before I can answer, your words turn into stones and plummet to the earth, where the snow greedily receives them.

Last winter we saw a train, which we didn't report, its polished brass fixtures smoldering in the early afternoon light. You wanted to sit in the lounge car, drink magenta wine from a crystal glass. You wanted to travel to the next town, where the proprietor of the mail order outlet had said that he had what you were looking for, a corset in which you exchange your dreams with a tenant from another century.

Behind us, a chorus of wolves began materializing on the ridge, something they learned from watching their brethren in the movies. Forced by the frost to wear their best sheepskin coats, they had only one goal in mind: Deflect the ghosts still floating untethered in the atmosphere.

How do I know all this? Perhaps because I am the figure others see tramping through the snow, the one whose cigar pokes holes in the sky. And before you answer, consider what happened the last time you committed your words to something other than memory.

The Long Way Around

Tomorrow I will remember this, two blazing green eyes peering at you (or is it me?) from above a black furry prow culminating in jagged yellow teeth.

I am standing in the crumbling remains of a doorway, my back pressed up against the last moments of a dying sun. This, the sign proclaims, is another perfect example. Of what, it neithers says nor points to. I take out my pencil, my camera, and my flask of purified river water. One of these, I am sure, will register this moment for posterity and that inevitable moment when my posterior outweighs the rest of my body.

My former neighbor, an ex-druggist, keeps a record of each time smoke interrupts her line of sight. Two bottle rockets from firehouse window on north side. Blue-haired man burping behind a string of green soap bubbles. But now is not the time to go further into these details, as there are others that are more pressing.

Yes, we came out here to look for the castle the bearded beer baron claims to have had shipped from the expanding waist (or middle) of California. Reading the glossy brochure we picked out in our hotel lobby this morning, we learned that a crew of tall but nearsighted masons had carefully numbered everything, from the rough granite stones and weathered wooden gates, to the priceless bric-a-brac that generations of previous owners had carefully arranged on polished shelves, in lacquered cabinets, behind squares and triangles of imperfect glass.

The drive is smooth and pleasant, and there are fewer packs of wild dogs the further we travel away from the horizon, its surprise of darkening red or what one writer called "the fatal bloom." Perhaps I should tell you what's on my mind, but I am not sure that there is anything there that could be construed as a thought or even thinking.

Do you feel this way often? Why yes, now that you mention it, I do. Sort of like licking a bowl that was empty long before you ever sat down, fork in one hand, spear in the other.

Speaking of spears, do you remember if we passed the pet cemetery or not? I think we might be headed in the wrong direction, not back to where we started out, but towards that place from which we never leave. The one that we resemble right down to the hair circling our increasingly inflamed snouts.

D ouble-Headed Creature Features

"Cold omelette," he told me, after coming down from the attic filled with ancient lanterns, "like big fish out of small sea, does not improve with age. Best to throw night nurse back into ditch of boiling shoes."

Remember, the use of words and phrases the audience has trouble translating is a quick way of introducing the real subject. Play up the foreign. For example: "Long bouts of feverish propagation are very popular among my kind."

Resist hankering. Acts of futility are preferable to scenes of fussiness.

You might also consider monocles for the third eye or (as they say where I or my twin come from) "medicated bullet." Authorial intrusions of this sort make excellent excerpts for doctoral candidates wishing to write about the restoration of restoration tragedies.

Items from wardrobe: burlap execution jacket embroidered with sinister signs; deformed slippers made of unfamiliar animal skins.

Don't forget accented touches possible with make-up; caterpillar eyebrows, well-oiled moustache, pencil line lips.

The wardrobe is necessary to successfully engineer the walrus walk, a gait that suggests slipperiness encased within a ponderous and solitary bulk, a figure alone with its wavelength of misbroadcast thoughts. Momentary glimpse of hairless body like those you see reflected in imported sunglasses. Usually appears shortly after words stick to bloody windshield.

As the perpetrator of other dastardly hoaxes, many with far reach consequences, Mr. Chang—or is it "Fang" or "Chain"—are you willing to speak in the most precise and tender terms known to emerge from a body burdened with a purple tongue?

"But is this not why I asked you to beat me with a borrowed broom?"

"Foolish rooster who stick head in lawnmower end up in concrete stew."

"Yes, but turtle in pond no more safe than dog glued to horse."

Once she enters the stables on the other side of the

crumbling bridge, its art nouveau silhouette flowing into a row of symmetrical flames licking the sky's feverish hair, the heroine delivers fatal punches to two drug-addled horses—note absent dogs—before knocking out three security guards who happen to be both half wits and half brothers, but, also, in a dream she had had many years ago, she remembers waiting on a table in a restaurant named *Honolulu Hanky Panky*. The menu included "Flaming Volcano Rocks" and "Lava Palaver Syrup," large square plates containing food blocks whose names, like master criminals, managed to elude her.

It was because of a lapse in memory that a baby-faced goon lost part of his leather-bound hand, while his vagabond cousin vanished into the poisonous bushes planted discreetly behind the blood-colored pool.

Ruby, a woman known for her collection of ruby earrings, leans forward and whispers to a suspicious-looking bartender (note tattoo of stolen car on chest): "So seldom do brains and beauty dance naked in the street together with the prisoners of fortune." All the seats behind her, save one, are empty. And maybe even that one is really casting the crenellated shadow of a false eyelash on the sand dune backed up against the far wall, beneath a puce colored ceramic ceiling, one burned-out bulb danging from a frayed wire covered with fake dead flies.

Circling the entrance to the parking lot of the *Vampire Hotel*, where the sign reads, "One Night's Sleep Feels Like An Eternity," the young couple listens to a man announce their impending arrival. Entertaining mayhem is about to occur along the crest of a smoke-laden ridge. In the basement of the temple, a fleet of tuxedoed rats elects a new savior, more shiny and handsome than the last one, who snuck aboard a cruise ship destined for Goa. Where lovelorn means a new chorus line every evening.

The Story So Far, and Not One Step Farther

A newly indentured driver is able to veer his undented cab to a stop. The smooth, reflective vehicle turns, tilts, slides, settles. Wheels finally come to a halt, hearts begin to deaccelerate.

Inside, while kneeling on the back seat, a diminuitive man of uncertain age and profession stealthily presses his manufactured right ear against the cold, double-paned glass, a habit he began refining in the middle stages of his urban childhood. Sounds are rapidly sorted, provisional calculations made, strands of evidence registered in an easily transportable data bank. What is to be found, he wonders, amidst the constantly accumulating rubble? Without sufficient warning, his rebuilt motion sensors detect the first incoming blips of a story.

Depressed by the sudden change in atmosphere, two professors make a solemn pact; they will bury their heads in vats of waterproof cement. Their wives do not seem appropriately alarmed by this prospect of humiliation and embarrassment.

In the basement of their jointly built bombshelter the two men consider their options, embarrassment before their colleagues, their wives, or both.

As more hours settle near the bottom of the beaker, it becomes apparent that winter has decided not to retreat after all. All morning, onyx stars (or "black snow") fill the long ruts where sky's corrugated backdrop unfurls along city limits. In the late afternoon, crowds begin huddling in the aisles of the hospital's amphitheater, the largest, inhabitable hollow within the complex of interleaving buildings, towers and jetways.

A series of games are devised, the rules of which are never firmly decided.

Out past the ambulance barn, decaying broadcasts of nearly forgotten contests between man and beast penetrate the air with a series of almost intelligible mechanical murmurs.

Time, someone mutters, is thickening and stretching, its toxic tarpaulin beginning to grip the edges of things. Soon all entrances and exits will become off-limits. Soon three-fingered headless hobgoblins will use one of their fingers to gesture to us from their stolen podiums.

From the back of the auditorium, another voice enters the fray. Were the woodchucks wrong to be the first among us to set their retirement cabins on fire? It is hard to venture any kind of reasonable answer, because even the smoke and ashes have vanished by the time the volunteer firemen are able to arrive from another dimension, buckets of mud balanced on the crest of their shiny, handmade helmets.

We sit transfixed by the sight of ourselves turning to stone.

The Shortest Distance Between Two Walls

Although now creaking and rolling—repetitive motion syndrome has clearly taken its toll—the machinery of waves has outlasted its once in a lifetime guarantee. Illegally manufactured barbituates manage to keep the herds of cocker spaniels sedate. Properly treated, they make such comfy footwarmers for the elderly among us. Still, our seagull festooned galleon has been drifting for many centuries, and we are finally getting tired of canned tomatoes, wind cured beef, and speckled rain water.

The third assistant chef tells us that we repeatedly misattribute the actual sources of our food, and that the entire kitchen crew is convinced that we have started to lose our ability to discern subtle differences in textures and tonalities, but how can this be? We are still able to sit perfectly upright on the well-mopped deck, neatly arranged beneath our blue and yellow government issue blankets, and carefully count the mounds and morsels the crew has discreetly placed before us. Certainly, there is nothing to suggest that what we have been eating is anything but what we have been told we are eating.

Since not a hair of the wind is out of place, and all the clouds are clean shaven and freshly powdered, we can deduce that we are not so different from the local atmosphere so as to be locked out of its sunlit library. The windows, I have been meaning to tell you, need polishing, and the apple trees could do with a careful pruning. Meanwhile, a shotgun might help rid us of those pesky jays. Why have you started glancing at the opposite page? Is there something there that has caught your eye? A drunken pterodactyl perhaps? Someone standing naked in the doorway of print your eyes are starting to devour?

From time to time, we can see other boats in the distance, their passengers waving bright red bandanas and singing old tunes from the old country, so old it is probably dead and forgotten by now. That is about the only time that I realize I should have listened to you and stayed at home, been happy with the little boat the volunteer firemen happily installed in the fireplace, its pink sails buffeted by purple smoke rising toward the soot-ringed ceiling we once called "Heaven."

Did I tell you that my photograph appeared in the back pages of the sepia sky yesterday? Its resemblance

to me was uncanny, especially since I no longer pos-
sess any accurate likeness of myself and am forced to
rely solely on other people's good intentions. We had
just managed to safely pass a point of land called
"The Devil's Nose."

It seems that, despite all that has happened, I haven't
changed very much, just enough to recognize that
most people no longer wave when they scurry past
me in the street. This however happened yesterday
on my way to the drugstore. An old bearded sailor in
borrowed shorts tried to stop me and sing a song.
Who wants to listen to a man who must borrow
someone else's shorts in order to sing? I asked him to
no avail. He tried to convince me that his song con-
tained a message from you, but I knew he was mis-
taken. I hear your voice all the time, I told him, and
it's been years since you have said anything new to
me.

Summer Rental

Mrs. Trashbag was unable to come to any reasonable appraisal of what was standing in front of her temporary desk, just that the old man's upswept hair bore a striking resemblance to the sleeves of his pleated, plaid coat. Who, her numbered underlings in the storeroom were whispering, could have possibly had the urge to rip all the plastic flowers out of their imported sleeping jackets? Was it the same culprit that last weekend stole a dozen infected parrots from the east wing of the castle's library? These are the questions haunting the pockmarked halls of the old tavern down by the harbor. Later, morning's leftover light is marked "dismal" and sent to the laboratory, where a team of agents carefully sifts through the spokes and glare.

The crew has gathered near where evening's shadows thicken their fur in anticipation of the coming weather. Everyone else in the parking lot knows the movie is just an excuse to tell a bad story in livid colors. A woman caresses the knotholes of her wooden leg. Treefrog Pete practices swallowing a woolen scarf. Meanwhile, the actors and actresses trying out for the lead roles believe they will be able to revive the remainder of their careers.

Next to the parking lot, in a government funded home for semi-retired adolescents, the newly appointed director wonders who has been pissing in the umbrella stand. His secretary secretly covets contact with grated substances. In the cellar, a spotted paw defiles a garment made of coal.

Thick with snakes and headbands, a stricken aroma undulates through a broken window. Once you are apprehended, you are returned to your room, and left with a plate of hot wax. This is what we in the institution fondly refer to as "living beyond your beans."

A cow imitates a car and crashes into a telephone pole. Grackles shriek and wolves whimper, but Byron Trashbag continues dozing on the bottom of the ocean floor, the brute hours of enforced labor wriggling through his muscles. He had had the worms before, but not like this. It is the month when penalties must be paid and extra facial hair removed from offending surfaces, the month when last year's prisoners are lowered into the lower bunkers, and music hour consists of the same insurgent anthem repeatedly played backwards.

The ambitious assistant director heard himself

announce to the seagulls still glued to the eaves of the burning roof: Once you've mutilated the night in your sleep, there is no turning back.

Summer Hiatus

Another scream is being carefully rehearsed in the lobby of this once famous hotel, though how it came to have a sterling reputation is no longer remembered, even by those who have been tenants since it first opened its monogrammed doors. Around noon, the gardener and his family arrive on a badly labeled bus. Not understanding the question, his mother, the president of the ant colony, once replied that she had often been compared to an oversized plant living at the bottom of an aquarium. In her old age, she wanted to be served a pitcher of iced bluegrass tea in the afternoon, down near where an earthquake had swallowed the scriptural highway. The birdbath needs cleaning. Someone has stolen the remaining umbrellas from the verandah.

Halfway down the grand staircase leading to the main ballroom, two centipedes approach me with their story. At first, one of them is extremely fidgety, and spends an inordinate amount of time adjusting each of his pink, seven-fingered, chamois gloves. The calmer one says he drives a red taxi on weekends, but I think this is a code for something else, something I am unable to decipher. The story they tell is not as simple as I initially guessed it would be, and it is voiced with barely acceptable levels of radiation. Eventually, tiring of the detours and delays, they order their servant, a worm of suspicious origin, to begin the long trek for a perfect martini.

A man in a wrinkled cigar hat begins examining the mold sprouting in the grooves of his cardboard legs. Why listen to the mournful crooning of old dogs and their oldest tricks? I possess far better things that I can launch, the man with a rectangular ruddy face covered with shorts dabs of repellent growth, earnestly announces.

She said that he was found at the bottom of a well, but it wasn't clear whether or not he was the painter we were looking for, the one who extracted vast cities out of dust.

According to the travel guide, he boiled eggs because he considered their shape to be perfect.

If I had known that it would come to this, I would have listened to my astrologer, who is known throughout the tri-county area for being right about half the time.

Did I mention the elderly sailor in a ragged fur collar,

his talking dog was still pointing at a row of blind-folded men and laughing. Most of the side streets were clogged with sand. Have you noticed that the sky smells of roofing tar?

P oem Based on a Non-Existent Photograph

S tanding on the steps of the main Branch Library of Unknown Occult Practices, knowing he is unable to gain entrance to the Archives of Necrophiliac Migrations, and their maze-like Hall of Disputed Testimony, he wonders whether or not to photograph the arrival of a large spotted blue butterfly on the nose of the granite sphinx, as he is convinced this encounter is an omen of some sort.

If he transfers the omen's momentary appearance to the realm of durable images, which he could later reproduce and sell at county fairs, would he have to report his dubious earnings to the Council of Elders or its subsidiary branch, the Clubhouse of Angry Offspring? Moreover, would those who buy the photograph and bring it into their apartments and trailers, their walkups and climb-ins, be subject to the omen's ominous forecast?

He is, of course, convinced that all omens are

ominous, that this is why they rhyme. He believes that in rhyme one catches a glimpse of the future, though he doesn't yet know he believes this, not having caught up with the wind, which is waiting for him in the doorway of a boarded-up government office building.

Or, in taking the photograph, would he be contaminating this zone of crystalline light inhabited solely by insect and stone, thus deflecting it into an area populated by the bilge beginning to clog the lake around which the city stretches.

He blinks. All is gone, the library a smoldering campfire, a row of footprints vanishing into a sandy gray sky.

He remembers that in his dream (or was it his fourth ex-wife's nightmare?), one of the offspring, Silk Chauffeur III, was photographed running through the police headquarters's parking lot for repeat offenders. Was he imitating a runaway milktruck, complete with perfect torsos dry and gleaming in the factory corrupted light? Or was he just another well-meaning muffin goober on the path to becoming an inebriated armadillo?

Boys love to chase armadilloes. Didn't he once read that in an issue of a science journal devoted to armor plated creatures?

Point of view, the instructor informed him, is important to maintain throughout a narrative.

He stood up and told the class that Mr. Chauffeur III had on an embroidered blue shirt, moth eaten around the area of his left nipple, which was pierced with a necklace of doll's teeth.

He then recounted the tale of Mr. Chauffeur's father, who was said to possess certain powers. For example, it is commonly accepted that the man who, early last winter, photographed Chauffeur's youngest son *in flagrante delicto* for a underground gossip kiosk, fell into an upscale uptown fish tank and became a pearl lodged in a famous diver's custom-made rubber glove.

Uniformed groups of ultra-superstitious gymnasts stop and consult the steady stream of bubbles rising to the oily surface. Silkscreened prayer mats, hand-kerchiefs and scarves are sold by throngs of street vendors, many of them citizens of distant lands.

> *Many of them more distant than others.*
> *One is known for its prefabricated chalets.*

Near the entrance to the small building containing the sacred fishtank, the head vendor, the leader of the Union of Carts, Catheters, and Caterers, sings to a small group of adoring admirers. One of the admirers has decided to move up the ladder of opportunity. (Here we might add is another thread the film could follow if the director finds he is getting too caught up in the existence of supernatural forces and thinks perhaps a few earthly delights might do the trick).

The sky is beginning to thicken behind the window of yesterday's soup. He wonders if the owner of the second-hand lingerie shop would remember him from the previous weekend. He had stood in the doorway opposite her front door and, using a tele-photo lens, taken photographs of her clientele, the men, women, children, and costumed pets entering and leaving the temporary dressing room. He told himself he was on a secret assignment. He was partic-ularly interested in the narrow figure that emerged from a hooded raincoat dressed as a nun. Would this figure return? he wondered. Was it another omen he shouldn't have recorded?

The more pressing concern was the dilemma regard-ing subject matter. Why had he turned his back, if that's what he did, on those moments of stillness that manage to crawl under the door?

Three eroded gas pumps herded beneath a flock of stars.

An oxidized storage tank mounted by a blue satellite dish.

Spindly limbs crowned by tufted wings.

And what was the meaning of the message, clearly intended for someone else, that was left on his answering machine?

"This is Poodle. He likes to write poems about muffins and pudding. Perhaps you will invite him deep into the Texas of your home and heart. As he is a somewhat damaged creature who was fitted with two extra feet and finds it understandably difficult to master the fine art of orthography, perhaps you will take up the pen on his behalf. Meanwhile, we here at the Clubhouse of Angry Offspring want to thank you for your recent portrait. It fits neatly into the envelope we are returning to you, along with a small but handsome gift. Don't give it another thought though, as it's not too small and not too handsome."

Our Small but Perfect Town

We used to be known for our carpets and calligraphy, our refrigerators and slippers, though for a long time that is all we were known for. We used to collect nails and other people's correspondence. We used to have strict rules about which fingers one could use to stab pieces of cooked food floating in the festive bowls full of ceremonial oil. Now we are allowed to speak freely on all matters, big or small, as long as we understand that our words will never be reflected in the municipal swimming pools clustered by the bus station.

We are notoriously slow to accept wonderful views of the mountains, even when they are comparable to a free policy of foolproof life insurance. Thus, we feel little need to venture down certain walks of public life, preferring instead to stay huddled over damaged cars and broken bicycles. Because time passes through our city like a lizard, no one has ever bothered to fix the clocks. They aren't even right twice a day.

The Difference Between Autobiography and Romance

I hand you a bottle of colorless ink that has fallen from the ceiling, its stucco clouds. A canoe drifts towards a deserted pyramid, its late summer shadow turning to elephant dust in the pockets of those standing in the wings and watching. We were able to leave the others when the weather pattern shifted toward a hallway connecting one part of the labyrinth to another. The curtains parted. As far as we could see, which wasn't very far, water was being excavated from the veins of the collapsed sky, its coal blue streets supported by sealed storerooms and ancient scaffolding.

In the second and final chapter chapter, flocks of red and yellow cows collect under the river, its staircase majestically rising toward a roof of hammered tin stars. The landscape of a dot circles beneath a moon of many dots. Some travelers have unpacked their box lunches near the sky's enameled feet.

Finally, our mouths begin wandering when we stop outside the Hall of Previous Enlargements, which our ancestors once used to impress others before visiting them. We realize that the ritual of exchanging digitally enhanced photographs has become a paper plane burning above our scattered memories. Perhaps this is when I should tell you that I used to live across the park from your chimneyed tent. But right now, the smudges are piling up between us.

The Dog and Pony Opera

I carry a large stash of perforated repro-ductions of forged vendor's licenses, which give the coveted bearer the right to sell:

A) a well-mannered, highly fetishized suc-cubus on any thoroughfare between the hours of midnight and the moment when the sun first grasps the horizon's foetid throat

B) talking and dancing dogs from a part of Siberia where talking and dancing is forbidden, especially among dogs

C) a bus pass good for buses in Singapore, Macao, and Kowloon, but not Hong Kong

D) a bus steering wheel that was made in Hong Kong

It wasn't always this pleasing, the morning full of tepid water flowing through the walls. I used to have to pretend that I was an orchid left on a schooner.

Outside the executioner's summer cottage, I tugged

at the sleeve where I was told an arm of enormous length once dangled. The bell sounded like an insomniac's nightmare. I couldn't remember if I was looking for a tattoo of a snake clutching an eagle or a three eyed monster peering out from under his mother's four poster bed. Do you remember which little horse I rode in on?

Whenever we had the chance, we read the local newspaper, though we didn't always understand it. The items listed under *Police Blotter* imparted the most pleasure, one we sipped slowly throughout the morning. The international edition was a more sobering encounter. As for the rest of the periodicals, they proved to be pesky, recurring fiascos we trained ourselves to ignore. Something like this had happened earlier in our journey, when we we were forced to speak well of the fleas practicing jump rope in the folds of our imported hats.

That morning, the once renowned painter told his dwindling circle of friends that he was withdrawing from any further contact. It wasn't exactly a cold day in hell, but it was close enough. He turned and left by the side door. By the time his friends went out into the street, to see where he had gone, snow had obliterated any footsteps he might have taken toward the horizons waiting at either end of the long narrow alley.

After we put two lit candles in the dead man's mouth, we proceeded in orderly fashion toward our initial goal, the *Happy Go Lucky* bus station near the center of town. According to the guide we found in the motel, the town was a honeycomb of opportunities burgeoning on the edge of a burly swamp known as Swamp Burly, named after a man whose family tree remains one of the mysteries that can still be found in our park. The expected slew of one-toothed guffaws fills a row of broken mugs. Before lighting an exploding cigar, the photographer counts the rest of his lucky stars. Who will tell him his wife's best friend is in love with the sudden appearance of smoke?

Most of the street signs are pointed in the right direction. Our electrical cord eyesight hasn't failed us. We stopped and bent forward, three worm-eaten prows cutting across the Arctic. We learned that the bus station was closed for minor repairs, so we did as we were instructed and drifted quietly downstream, to the platform in front of a jewelry store whose owner has recently run off with his wife's prize turtles. It began raining, small tasteless drops at first, like the kind you might find tucked away in a hardware store full of software. This interlude seemed important, a time to make further amends or state your latest wishes.

Categorical imperatives are not required, but, over long weekends, suits and ties are occasionally requested by the company comptroller.

Not wishing to ignore the favorable signs mounted in the outer lining of the overcast sky, we told each other that we hadn't planned to rob the bank that morning, that it was something that happened to us while we were standing there, waiting to try the free samples they were offering their loyal customers. Having been raised by a pack of rabid wolves, we know something about loyalty and what it tastes like when you are thirsty and crawling through a dirty parking lot. Spotlights sweep the sticky asphalt, while underpaid guards free the centipedes and rehearse unlikely scenarios, their favorite being battle weary formations of heavily armed primates storming the castle gates.

The dead man pretended that he had been shot by an overzealous intruder named Maximum Detail. Except for the marshal's droopy, three-legged hound, no one seems to come close to fitting the description. Such gaps allow us to press on with the story we had been told by our abductors to deliver. The sky grows green and newly minted clouds drift out over the rat infested plains.

I 'm just a Factory Boy

Men make the clothes, with needles and pins stuck through their briny tongues and red scalloped cheeks, and bright thick yellow thread wound tightly around their right ears. Always cocked nervously towards the regulation sized windows, their dusty blue waves of unnameable particles and flakes, their left ears remain, of course, unencumbered by any of the by-now familiar mementoes of time's indigo horns. The sound of hands and feet accomplishing their appointed tasks fills the currents of circulating air with a comforting lullaby of old meanings, some of which have been forgotten.

Often, at night, after leaving the old bar I visit down by the edge of the deserted harbor, I return to the circular stainless steel stairs leading to the factory. I sneak in through the open window I arranged earlier in the day and sit at my station. I begin humming a popular tune from another era, one which I myself didn't witness.

Do you remember the day we were accosted by snakes? The ones in front were waving thick banners and shouting foreign slogans. Someone told us that they were protesting the caterpillars's increasingly militant interest in the safe arrival of the future. We stopped and looked at the flowers, delicate as snowflakes, cluttering the lawns. The scent of thick slices of lemon cake drifted across the timorous lake. The rest of the afternoon was punctuated by the sound of a motorized pizza oven being open and shut. The whine of its door was a kind of music.

On a narrow stone escarpment of the castle overlooking town, three rotund grasshoppers are holding their weekly meeting. One of them wants to mention an obituary he read in the morning newspaper. The deceased, it seems, spent a large part of his life thinking and reading. According to the reporter, the handful of unaccounted periods in the deceased's long and productive life amounted to nothing more than a terraced receptacle jutting out from one corner of the room.

S*econd*
Chapter

And then the painter, having rubbed much too much pigment into the fissures already spreading beneath the first layers of the previously assembled sky, known among the villagers as the "Absolutely Absent Tenant," stopped and watched its stained and crumbling pages rise toward the trellised window, its view of the unbundled stars.

She turned and told him that she had held nothing, not even the faintest glimmer, back, even if later she didn't remember what she had said, it was what came to her, the turbulent sky fleeing her mouth, everything in the forest turning to greet it.

When her lips stop imitating the fishnet sky, she finds it is necessary to kneel down and rub a lamp of dirt to learn which colors are supplemental. There is nothing supernatural about this, it is simply a ritual she conjured up one morning while preparing to sail to another city.

125

The castle and prince are sideline spectators, bunched folds collapsing into flames dancing around the mirror in which she sees her face, a statuary profile, shed its silvery skin. In the foreground, the shadow of a jagged chimney someone in the backseat points at, and describes in two languages, as you are carried swiftly towards the water's scalloped edge.

Side Street Adjacent to Lower Breughel Parkway

After emerging from the maelstrom that had threatened for days to take over the barnyard, the painter said the rest of us would eventually stop oozing onto the sheaves of winter wheat.

Who was going to convince us that the villains would get what they deserved, a wheelbarrow full of poisoned meat? Dissatisfied with the painter's toothless assurances, we decided to take the very next Vermeer yellow bus back into town.

A voice penetrated the sheets of paper separating us from our shadows, those speckled lizards that follow in our footsteps. "This guy's just received a major endorsement to manufacture pails of soup. Only six per customer." Soon, we learned that Kurt wanted to go to the rat catching party in his dinosaur egg hat.

And then Sibyl pouted, and both Wanda and Rhonda kicked their gift parcels into the claws of the fire. Finally, the bus arrived, full of ants returning from a picnic by the landfill known as Albert's Lamp.

Later, as we passed the town of New Debt, those seated on the left side of the bus watched an Egyptian moon flood the far side of the lake with ballpoint pearls, while the view from the right side caused ripples of despair and panic to sweep out to the teeming black horizon and back again.

Even though his beard was infested with gusts of flies, and his dog was busy licking the neighbor's newly imported cutlery, the painter exuded a sunny confidence. Some of the taller ones among us got jealous. Guttural insults and grammatical growling could be heard rising toward a break in the clouds, but it was to no avail. His dog's disposition, however, was of the kind best deposited into a paper bag you try to discreetly drop beside a leering adult male.

After the president of the pheasants twice clangs his unshaven nugget against the butcher's sturdy barn, we know the radio signal has been received in the burning hut. Once again, we will become the toast of the townpeople. Still, we must fill our glasses with the knowledge that the utility birds will remain ignorant about live volcano acts. It is like living under an umbrella stapled to the rain.

If the truth (or its bird of hatching doubles) be known, my freshly dry cleaned, vintage Sumerian shirt isn't nearly as loud an abstract friction as you have claimed while we were rummaging through the new bodega of cellulite sufferering of every kind but ours.

Are we just another pair of bicycling brassiere leopards loosening vowels from their platinum lockets, cotton pockets, and electric sprockets?

Whose alphabet lifts consonants from the flames hordes of hairy hoboes have hauled across the buxom plains?

In a city where no one under a hundred-and-one is allowed to pee behind the marble benches, a custom we learned to enforce from our mother long ago, I send you this dirty little tourniquet of a song. Its tin can factotum factory rope is for you and your family of vibrating pumpkins. May the ledge be large enough for the remnants of the cyborg's brain.

Wasn't it only yesterday that I received its final transmission? Select me for your bird and beak machine if I am wrong, but didn't one of you just say you wanted to curdle long into the conjugated night?

The Annual Indoor Picnic of Ambulatory Somnambulists

One of us said that it would be best if all of us waited at the bullet-riddled sign directing wide-eyed pedestrians to the cobblestone street formerly known as *Bird in the Hand*, but another said it wasn't as convenient as being able to stand under the polka-dotted awning of the inn of divorce known as *Two in the Bush*. Although some of the fringe members in the back of the rented auditorium gestured wildly at heaven, which, as usual, did not bother replying, the meeting went as smoothly as could be expected, given the diversity of our membership. No further rumors of insect warfare spread through the jowls of others present at our secret gathering. Then one of the figures on the upper shelves woke up and reported a more acceptable sighting.

It was decided that the main group would rendezvous

in front of *The Sacred Cow*, a dairy-free vegetarian restaurant in a quaint sundrenched neighborhood near where we often pass each other without stopping, but this proved more difficult than the planning committee predicted. The streets and shadows we so looked forward to reentering had been folded into the nooks and crannies of what replaced them, a city-state of unknown origin, bad food, and poor planning. Understandably, its citizens did not announce their allegiance to another flag. They liked to claim that they didn't find such declarations of improvidence necessary.

In a small but seemingly well-known though not particularly popular bar named *Repository of All Your Worthless Sorrows,* we sat to one side, drinking from goblets shaped like dented grasshoppers. As we were not sure that this was where we were supposed to be sitting, it didn't take too long before dismay entered the picture. We began pleading our case. We had imagined a gold-trimmed balcony, not seats close to the sawdust and fermenting piss. None of the explanations we were able to construe possessed the proper ratio of meticulousness to randomness. Had time's witness rejection program acceletrated its processing center? Or was it simply that our own age had not only caught up with us, but had also passed us by?

Even though none of us had received the application form, we were pronounced unfit for the School of Prospective Gentlemen and their Well-Behaved Pets. We kicked both ourselves and each other for not growling more at our well-rested neighbors.

The clouds posted banners stamped with the phrase "accumulate cumulus for a rainy day."

Three rows of different-sized triplets polished the lower corners of the salamander sky.

Henry, which was the name you were using that afternoon, spoke first: "Does it matter if we don't find what we are looking for? Perhaps what we find in its place, which obviously was a vast and thorough illusion to begin with, will offer delights undreamed of by us in the sheds of our former existence, the ones whose dimensions fail to fit neatly around our skin."

I wanted to argue with Henry but I couldn't. Another voice, its shadow, had spilled across mine. Not able to speak, I could only listen to what I was saying: "After I threw away my suit, I took a walk into the mountains. There I found a piece of chalk. This is how I began my nights as a ragamuffin, a coffee cake bandit complete with toffee-colored bandana. Did you place flowers on all the errors we made, the ones with consequences and the ones without applause?"

The Unexpurgated Biography of Simon Yam

for Garrett Caples and Anna Naruta

A swarm of motorized yellow flies hovers above the well-plotted, well-groomed outskirts of an immense tunnelled city known as Nameless Entity. Two quick flicks of a grooved cog followed by low level chatter and languid snickering. Another row of mute reflections shattered by the sound of imaginary gunfire. Gatehouse, gashouse. Any order we might derive from language isn't based on the alphabet.

Will Mister Goon kindly rise from the comfortable declivity of his black canvas chair and introduce himself to Mister Drizzly, who currently finds himself surrounded by a battalion of unemployable shepherds?

A pile of expired writing machines, their sleek innards glittering in the artificial moonlight.

No roamers or deluded sycophants spotted on the digital grid.

Collective pulse rate maintained at a level just below boiling.

It's Monday morning, which the President has twice failed to declare National Pedestrian Day. The smell of crocodile piss rises past the thirty-ninth floor of the retired skinflints's highrise, where, on an extra large, post-minimalist balcony facing the remnants of Portuguese colonialism, two primordial simians argue over a pot of rubber chrysanthemums.

Wilkie Collins licks the nib of his pen, so sweet and delicious.

In the kitchen a voice stuck inside a radio complains about having to face bulging testicles while seated on a city bus.

A preserved paw from an unknown species rolls noisily across a polished teak table.

A cliff face of sharply breaking clouds is reflected upside down in the baby-faced gangster's red Italian car's windswept windshield as he spins through the octopus lanes encircling Hong Kong.

Boxes of pills neatly stacked like lascivious elephants in tight Hawaiian shirts doing the forbidden hula.

It is reported that Little Fatty McDonough liked to stroll with his terrier Paddy O' Peaches on the diamond dust sidewalk in front of Pharoah Pharmaceuticals and Pyramid Farm Insurance.

It is before midnight there, but a little cylinder of mist drifting past midnight here, she whispers into the phone shaped like a shiny, bare-all, high heeled shoe, circa 1932, the year Anna May Wong boarded a train leaving Shanghai in a backlot in Southern California. She was barely twenty-five and old enough to cross the western plains in a thickly draped, private club car alone.

Without having to wrap grapefruit in party-colored condoms and then insure and ship them to South Kalamazoo, where mangy denizens of the privately funded zoo seem to find an unrepeatable delight buried in the stringy seams of their succulent sections, I am as likely to be called Dutch Holland, ex-president of the Crumpled Bag Society or Shamefully Nameless Entity, which is not to confused with a nearly likewise named city rumored to exist underground.

Whatever we do to each other tonight will have to be done in words we haven't used before. Otherwise the stainless steel bowl we lick will be full of amber.

Did I tell you that the people crammed into the milk truck going through the parking lot of the incendiary manufacturer's subsidiary research and development lab are sad, because unrelenting streams of sadness are much less expensive to obtain than little bundles of happiness, which can cost as much as two dozen chickens and a child's new rocket ship and docking station?

First I stole your pillow, and then I stole your pillow case, because I wanted the whole story, not just the bed on which the mockingbird nests. Was it only just yesterday that I smelled the trail of you that left with the others? Or will that happen tomorrow now that I been elected to be one of the many others and was told by my superior to make sure that the sky remains hard, blue and empty?

U*ntitled and Unnumbered*

Their original mission no longer a necessity on the remnants of what was still known as "the world stage," a squadron of aviators began circling a volcano they found plunked on a geometrically shaped mass of frenetic curdling. The youngest pilot, convinced that this is his best, and perhaps only chance to document his glorious plummet into history's silvery maw, that mythical volume some of the best libraries still claim to possess, began transmitting the first of his many visions.

Burnt bulbs are plucked from the marquee and italicized words scroll past, while the latecomers are finally able to settle comfortably into their warm buckets. Yesterday, we paused before a signet sky flanked by charred columns and porches rising toward rafts of chatter. A sky-infested flag lifted its declaration above a supermarket where muddy centaurs gripped bugles. This morning we started swimming out to meet the clouds sent here from that other world.

Three Panels from an Anonymous Fifteenth-Century Painting Which Has Been Subsequently Repainted on Two Occasions

Icky, Sticky, and Velcro belong to a band of renegade weasels. Today, beneath a cool and cloudy peachfuzz spread, they don peacock hats and cowboy moustaches, and head toward the seamiest side of town, its circle of tiled warehouses. They are looking for a kilim reputed to be imprinted with trails of cloudy blue semen from their magician ancestors, Saint Wicky and Aunt Nicky. According to the ancient illuminated treatise that they have managed to wrest away from their arch-enemies, the Hazelnuts, possession of the rug ensures that none of the owner's heirs will end their days as an uninsured chauffeur to Baron Iron Will, scourge of chauffeurs and weasels throughout the kingdom.

For many years the Baron has periodically returned in the morning minus his chauffeur. The same story accompanies this recurring event. Shortly before the dawn, the chauffeur asks if he can stop the royal limousine by the side of the road, pardons himself, and goes into the woods to relieve his bulging bladder, never to be seen or heard from again. A few days later his chapeau is discovered by a hunting party, dangling from a broken branch, as if it had been forgotten by someone suddenly in a hurry.

The Baron is short and square; he likes to squat when he speaks. He derives his iron grip from circumstances he has come accept as a material message delivered by fate, its borrowed chariot. Whenever he passes a full-length mirror, he reminds himself that the ivy covered tower bearing his family crest controls the narrow pass leading to and from this hillside enclave. The world doesn't revolve around him, but it might as well. For nearly ninety-nine decades, or the average lifespan of a stuffed weasel, his family has been celebrated for their confetti, which they produce in a variety of colors, textures, and shapes. A free sample is available to anyone who buys a dozen or more boxes of the Baron's new product, *Infinity's Fireworks*.

Three Wheel Rocket

As further evidence of our growing spiral towards signs alluding to one's physical girth, the saboteur pointed discreetly at a neatly engraved placard in a bookstore window:

"You don't have to be potbellied to enjoy the latest potboiler."

In the grassy foreground, two greasy mandrills gleefully mashed the red iron potatoes decorating a mandolin player's hand-me-down platter.

Oversized hooves detonate near the backdrop of wooly mountains.

Copycat screams of a blood-curdling nature gather beneath heaven's frayed and cloudless canopy.

Virginal in every respect but one, though not necessarily the one you—the infinitely suspicious reader—are thinking about, because that it is your inescapable inclination, your ticking brain at work, the hairless young emperor patiently circled his gilded encyclo-pedia, looking for a more appropriate encomium to deliver to those waiting to gather on either side of his narrow, slippered feet.

Yesterday, over possum pudding, his grand vizier told him that he had recently acquired incon-trovertible proof that the sky had been conquered by oval relics.

According to scientific reports, the stars are no longer viable as reading matter.

Remembering the future's outer face is one kind of protection against fraud. Copying its fingerprints is another. Apparently this is different than scissoring a slice of excavation from doom's faceless mirror. Or, after throwing twelve body-like stones into the filtering fire, waiting for the flame's black teeth to spew out tidings of what is to come. A rosette window faces east, towards the room where after-noon's pinkish gathering of smoke hoists its noose above *The New New Cathay*, a coffined snowdrop frequented by murmuring lemurs who like to loaf near the padded shelves lining *Ye Olde Butterfly Lounge*.

Among the kitchen colonnades, trays of thin-stemmed, sapphire-colored glasses salivate over the prospect of what awaits them, perfectly molded facsimiles of lips unhurriedly withdrawing from the precincts of intimacy and corruption.

I have been hired to slip through the side door because only one side of me is visible, a fuzzy yellow kangaroo badge facing an unsettled past occupied by you and three other vehicles of infamous recollections.

We are destined to meet in a moment adjacent to this one, a hotel room complete with towels and leather straps.

A list of new diseases has been tacked to the door.

Meanwhile, in the cavernous foyer, an ancient movie projector's craggy gargoyle gargles steadily, but, bending and falling, its traceries of light are unable to firmly press themselves against the wall reserved for moments like these.

A flock of stabilized limbs offers round-shouldered pedestrians small black roses.

Two recently housebroken cowpokes keep scurrying over the statues of their long-maned horses because what they are looking for resides out of necessity on the other side of a large and jittery obstacle.

On the rolling valley's hermaphrodite cranium, where shadows sway like a yacht's chandeliers, a spotted wagon carries a bevy of fur-bedecked revelers through the first of night's many vast and vacant lots. An infinitely bisectable plane over through and around which hungry prides mindlessly migrate.

On the northern border of an illegally subdivided, mid-sized, squarish plot marked "Available for Indispensable Inquisitions," close to where Old Mister Ocean is said to have risen from his bumpy bed, scores of children investigate their clothes for signs of impending danger.

In a towerless town of small distinction,

dawn bobs and weaves around an invisible foe. The thrice retired mayor jots down the first hieroglyphs of his memoir, *The Nourishing Power of Spiritual Greed*, while his children glide effortlessly between the trees, looking for sacks of contraband.

For the cowled pilgrims who, earlier in the labyrinthine corridors of time's disintegration, with a bite echoing the late regal style, stopped and stooped forward, to survey an artist's reasonably competent depiction of an immense wooded bay, it might one day be remembered by one of these travellers that the celebrated silhouette of *Thunderclap Lodge* is visible in the dead cowpoke's watery gray eyes.

On the bottom ledge of his glass eye's cloudy embrace three women can be seen busily planting blood-colored nails in the dew-soaked ashes of the smoldering dance hall.

Inside the toy spaceship bobbing above the clouds now starting to threaten the less-than-idyllic scene unfastening itself from the plains below, the surviving crew members pray that a giant claw will pluck them from the sky.

My Heart Is That Eternal Rose Tattoo

The ancient wooden wheel still turns close to the concrete dam, like a horse clomping its hooves beside a whirring motor. The rear doors of a shiny black post-war sedan open slowly. Three unrelated children of approximately the same size stop and stare at a well-groomed, spotted dog named Spotless. Nearby, two swimsuited matrons packing heavy artillery board the last commuter train to chug out of Bumblebee Flats, a small seaside resort known for its breezy golf course and aging adagio acts. What distinguishes these adagio acts from others is not the age of the performers, although many of them do collect pensions of one kind or another, but that none of them seems to have gotten a tattoo despite all the time they spent hanging around docks and wharves and gull-infested marinas.

Gladys is on what she believes is her final mission. On Monday, in a hotel near the central square of East

Turkey Hill, she will have the nearly orgasmic plea-
sure of plugging some more holes in her boss's delin-
quent halfwit cousin, Carl, who thinks he is only one
who knows he is having an affair with Glady's tall,
empty-headed sister, Arlene. Meanwhile, Arlene,
who is neither as tall as she would like to be, nor as
empty-headed as everyone likes to think she is, has
convinced her loud-mouthed, freckled nephew,
Cecil, that she has gotten herself stuck in a stagnant
marriage with Bill, Joey's younger brother.

In the next chapter, Joey, who is married to Heather,
the other woman who has boarded the train, realizes
that he is stuck on Regina, a young woman whose
tragic life is the basis of a novel which has received
uniformly negative reviews. However, in the highly
acclaimed film version, Regina's name is changed to
Gladys. In addition, the screenwriter introduces a
new character, Harold, who is a compilation of the
best traits of Cecil and Joey, while Heather becomes
an even more shadowy figure lurking in the dotted
background.

This is the chapter where I come in. For many years
I worked as a teller in the town's only bank. Each
morning I showed up promptly. Each evening I
pulled down the gate of my barred window, pushed
my chair back from the marble counter, gathered
myself into an erect form and departed the premises.
As I walked toward the exit, camel-hair coat
folded neatly over my left forearm, I gained a certain
satisfaction from knowing that the marble counter I
had just left was as smooth as the day it was hauled

down from the quarry, and that all the bills had been carefully rubbed before they were assigned to their proper sleeping quarters.

Throughout the long sun-filled days that infiltrated this small and ordinary town, I carried out all my designated duties with a reasonably serious smile. I petted children and talked to their stuffed animals. As instructed by the manual, I counted each fistful of bills the customers thrust at me three times. Always with my hands on the counter, in plain view. I never sneezed, never stopped to pull a handkerchief from my vest pocket. I was a neatly dressed, polite, some-what retiring man whose only sign of extravagance was feeding his turtles, Gladys and Heather, bits of raw sirloin obtained from the local butcher.

Now, as my eyesight worsens and my bones become more brittle, I want to ask you to tell me the story of your life. You see, I have grown tired of making addendums and adjustments, of tallying the stars that have been added to the sky.

Okay, maybe I just want to know if you remember the smell of wet hounds drifting into the diner, where a few hunters had gathered, that cold autumn morning long ago, when the sun still managed to rise gracefully above the harvest-colored mountains, and all our tears hadn't started filling tomorrow's stars to bursting.

Yes, you can have the rest of my cake. And yes, you can eat it, too.

VI

From Obit to Possible Epitaph

(James S. Moran 1907-1999)

for Bruce and Jean Conner

"It's a sad day for American capitalism when a man can't fly a midget on a kite over Central Park."

S*ingle*

Truncated predator seeks proof of paradisiacal paraphernalia. Failed nipple grievances at burly stage. Now raw tongue offends devotion. Specialty is furiousness of fur in sunset instances. Possesses metronome geniality but lacks basic dancing skills, the two-step platypus exceeding the hut of his mathematical abilities. Occasionally boasts of toasted gloves and other soap bubbles tossed on imperial porch. Impervious to lead and agave spiders crawling inside crook and nanny brain, its gelatinous rivulets. Built like a dusty armoire, complete with snakeskin-lined acoustic gully.

D*ouble*
Self-Portrait

Andrew Warhola changed his name to Andy Warhol because he wanted to be more American. He got his wish. Eventually he was called Andy by nearly everyone and was known as the Pope of Pop. Besides a love for Coca Cola, Andy had something else in common with the Presidents, with Jimmy and Ronnie and now Bill; he had a user friendly name.

Although he was once known as Mao Tse Tung, Mao Zedong didn't have to change his name to become more Chinese, and there was little he could have done to have become less Chinese. He was simply Chairman Mao, guiding light of the Chinese People's Republic. Mao and Jimmy and Ronnie shared something that Andy didn't have, the power to commute a death sentence.

Mao grew increasingly reclusive as he got older, and for months there would neither be a public sighting of him nor an official photograph released to the press. He was an invisible but palpable presence, a kind of yellow ghost.

Andy often went to three or four parties an evening. People liked to stand next to him and be photographed. Mao didn't pal around with other heads of state. He didn't play golf with Ike, he didn't sip wine with Nixon or share borscht and a belly laugh with Stalin. Mao wasn't friends with either the Shah of Iran or Imelda Marcos, while Warhol wanted to be commissioned to do both their and their spouse's portraits.

At the height of his fame, Mao stared down from billboards, the walls of train stations, schools, and airports. He was ubiquitous, a portrait painter's dream.

Warhol was sure that a commissioned portrait of the Shah of Iran would lead to all the money that he had ever dreamed of having, that his portrait of the Shah would be displayed in every state building and official instituition. Iran wasn't as big as China, but it had a lot of bus and train stations, post offices, hospitals, lobbies, rooms where bureacrats sat behind desks pretending to listen to whoever was speaking.

Mao liked to practice tai-chi as well as swim. Andy thought we would all be better off if we became machines. They were more efficient, shinier, and less likely to break down. According to photo analysts in the West, the official Chinese news photograph of

Mao swimming in the Yangtze River was fabricated, most likely to prove the Chinese leader was in good health. Andy was a hypochondriac, Mao was a septugenarian.

Warhol once had a double or stand-in give a lecture for him. It was part of his machine aesthetic, the human seen as an object that can be both interchanged and replaced by a perfect likeness. A number of observers thought that the fabricated photograph was proof that Mao was dead. Warhol once told his assistant that they could leave the party at which they had only just arrived, because someone had taken their photograph when they were standing in the foyer. This meant that everyone would know that they had been there.

Mao was the postwar embodiment of the Yellow Peril, the latest manifestation of Genghis Chan and Fu Manchu. Warhol preferred to negotiate his urban environment in a yellow cab.

Mao issued five year plans to inspire the masses, as well as to raise the level of production by both factory workers and farmers. He wanted China to make the "Great Leap Forward" and enter the modern age. Warhol hired someone to keep track of all the money he spent. He called her every day.

Mao started the Cultural Revolution. Warhol is said to have brought about "The death of painting," a bourgeois art form Mao approved of when it suited him.

Mao said, "Let a hundred flowers bloom, Let a hundred voices speak." But within a short time, he changed his mind. He sent intellectuals into the countryside to be re-educated. A few years later Andy Warhol and his assistants applied swirling fields of fuschia blush, hot pink, emerald green, and royal violet to a silkscreened reproduction of Mao's smooth rotund face. He would make Mao a ubiquitous presence in certain institutions, none of which were train stations.

Warhol grew up up near Pittsburgh, which, in the 1930s, was not famous for its Chinese restaurants. Warhol, who didn't like to eat, liked Chinese food well enough to be seen in a Chinese restaurant in New York run by Michael and Tina Chow. The Chows commisioned Warhol to do their portraits. There are many photographs of individuals seated or standing in front of their silkscreened portrait by Warhol.

Had Warhol been born in Los Angeles, his mother would have taken him to Graumann's Chinese Theater where he would have learned that not all Chinamen wear drab suits named after them. Some wear pigtails. Some of them iron men's shirts. And some wear robes with big sleeves, where one can hide a knife or bamboo blowgun. All of them talk funny and mispronounce certain English words. Warhol often chose to be silent because he remembered how badly his parents spoke English.

Warhol wrote fan letters to the child stars Shirley

Temple and Mickey Rooney. Mao issued directives and exhortations to the people.

Warhol's many different colored versions of the same impassive image suggest that he thought of Mao as a cash cow, a money tree, or wishing well.

What seems like a complete set of Mao prints is mounted in the wainscotted waiting room of *Art in America*. A dozen different colored versions of the same face stare down, a parody of the little one-room school and the reproduction of George Washington presiding over the children. Are we to construe absolutely nothing from Warhol's Mao? Looking at the different colored faces, is it just a pleasant (or unpleasant) art experience, a warm little buzz?

Because Mao always looks like himself, does that mean all Chinese look alike?

Had these two men, one a pope and the other the leader of the Red Army, ever met, would Warhol have told Mao that he should go to a better tailor, maybe in Hong Kong where tailors fitted the client with silk? Would he have asked Mao about his sex life, something he always tried to get Elizabeth Taylor to talk about? Would he have given him a copy of his magazine *Interview*?

Suppose Mao didn't like silk because it reminded him of the decadence and corruption of China's past? Suppose he didn't think talking about his sex life would help make him become more of a figure of intrigue and gossip?

Warhol tried to change his past by claiming he was born in Newport, Rhode Island. He once told someone that his mother gave birth to him during a fire.

Although one was a dictator and the other was an artist, both men were authors and thus predisposed to lying.

Each is remembered for his pithy observations which became clichés that others continue to quote. Everyone gets their "Fifteen minutes" and power comes from the "barrel of a gun."

They have been three, four, six, nine, and thirteen letter answers in crossword puzzles.

Caption to a Postcard from the 20th Century

The municipal parking lot finally reaches the horizon.

C*hinese Spoke*

I'm writing a letter before you board the plane. I'm writing a letter while the bells are sleeping. I'm writing a letter to my older brother who died before I was born. I'm talking to my adopted shadow on the phone. I'm whispering to a lieutenant or a nurse. I'm taking a roll of pictures of a young girl whose father sleeps in a ninety year old museum. I'm watching the sun rise over bandages, blankets, and umbrellas, all neatly stacked and numbered. I'm washing the thickest sections of my face. I'm drawing a picture of a man who monitors the mining industry. I'm interviewing a surgeon about his worship of cats and belief in the afterlife. I'm putting on the clothes I stole from a library. I'm reading a book about planes, locomotives, and washing machines. I am assembling a newly created deciduous plant which comes with a lifetime guarantee. I'm doing nothing better than I did before.

C*hinese Spoke (2)*

Please wait in this chair. Tell the story of the Canadian who couldn't remember the Chinese word for phone. There are fifty names on this list and yours isn't the only one with problems. Please walk into that room. Tell the story of the man who was afraid of his wife. I've already asked my brother to entertain you. Please draw a horizontal line that extends beyond the sky. Tell the story of the black shoes, white sandals and red rubber boots. Please swallow all of your food. I've already made an inspection. Please tell everyone the front of the building faces the stars. The weather has been a triangle of late, and you never know which side has decided to show up. Tell the story about the museum that had to sell its doors. From now on, please remember to always carry two suitcases, one for arrival and the other for departure.

A *Physical Matter*

Ogden Mushquick wasn't very fast, the world's plumed wagons having passed him by on more than one occasion. His physics professor marvelled at this phenomenon, one instance of time veering away from another, as if aghast at the prospect of meeting and mingling. Metamorphosis, Ogden told himself, wasn't in the cards. Other venues and openings would be denied him.

Yesterday, swathed in coats and scarves, Ogden took up considerable space on a park bench and waited. No one seemed to notice this oversized boy until the moon hoisted its indigo umbrella above his squat pimply oblong vertical bumpy projectile body squatting (like a misshapen dog he would later think) on pristine planks marked "Public Property."

Ogden had hoped to gain such a stamp, perhaps by mistake. Branded in this manner, he could put himself up for adoption; he could claim the government, certainly the mayor's office, had to tend to him. It would, he believed, make him desirable, a wanted thing. Such a mistake by a city worker was not, however, to be made, as two uniformed shadows shooed him away. But only after one of them giggled and the other sneezed.

Gas mask check, bandage count, water bottle level registered. Was there always some bodily eruption before he was spoken to? Some emptying and spewing? Was the officer's sneeze a harbinger of things to come? Ogden did not want to ponder the consequences of this likelihood, preferring to believe that the warranties in his possession were still good.

There was nothing else he could do but embrace the bumpy body that was his and his alone. He was all too familiar with the view that he wasn't fit for comparisons. As his mathematics teacher pointed out, a little too enthusiastically—the ragged cloud writing this down, might add—the other half of the equation always got a raw deal. He wondered why, as he was neither boisterous nor an oyster.

He could hear someone leaning out a jagged window, boiled sleeves flapping in the crosstown wind.

Who will clean up this spot of sky? Who will retrieve the wigs from the furnace?

As you might have guessed, I have been sitting by the window of this low-end diner for a long time. My eggs are empty hammocks, and the bacon is encased in a pleasantly-colored gel. I ignore the two men carrying shovels to the men's room. The cat remains inanimate, a ball of striped fur stuck to the bulletin board full of slips of colored paper, scribbled numbers, dotted faces, and printed addresses.

I don't let these details crowd my attention, force me to switch from one channel to another. I stare straight ahead, as if rereading the neon sign mounted on the roof; curving colored tubes glowing against a blackboard sky. I know something fishy is going on across the street, in the Mortician's Union. I just don't know what.

My whiskers twitch, the signals are faint but detectable.

The indelible ink is seeping into your eye, the glass one you keep in your pocket, a good luck charm I am told.

Perhaps, before taking any more notes, you will permit me the opportunity to tell you the story of a small puddle of a man who has eluded detection until now, if now is made up of all the times intersecting this one in which all the pronouns might be inhabitants. It was winter when it was first posted that I was missing. Seems I slipped through the drifting nets. Or is it the "I" that I once was wafted away, carried off by an invisible bird, preferably a black eagle, having become reconstituted into someone else. And that someone else, be it Ogden Mushquick, Nicodemus Wong, or Sap The Dripper, drove a sedan the color of a stormy sky on a north winter night said the witness who may or may not have been a witless accomplice, a non-stick windshield wiper, or fully refundable dog walker.

You have to get close enough to the head eraser to waste the lead with your tongue. This, the one of us that is on the far left is told, is the password that admits you into the tunnels of the ice house.

Once you are inside its varnished newspaper doors, and their headlines of unending disputes, you have to shed every strip of fur you have attached yourself to. Become, as the wooden sign says, a nondescript edifice, a barely balanced pile of stones waiting for history's sands to shift. And having come this far, you must now decide who is to say who is saying what might be of all the things said the things that should have been said above and beneath all others?

Printed December 2001 in Santa Barbara &
Ann Arbor for the Black Sparrow Press by
Mackintosh Typography & Edwards Brothers Inc.
Text set in Galliard by Sasha Newborn.
Design by Barbara Martin.
This first edition is published in paper wrappers;
there are 200 hardcover trade copies;
100 hardcover copies have been numbered & signed
by the author; & 22 copies lettered A–V
are handbound in boards by Earle Gray
each with an original artwork by John Yau.

Photograph by Eve Aschheim
Painting by Norman Bluhm

JOHN YAU was born in Lynn, Massachusetts, on June 5, 1950, shortly after his parents fled Shanghai. B.A. from Bard College, where he studied with Robert Kelly, and M.F.A. from Brooklyn College, where he studied with John Ashbery. Began writing about modern and contemporary art in 1978, and has written for most every art magazine, as well as contributed essays to many monographs and catalogs. Currently on the faculty of the Mount Royal Graduate School of Art (Maryland Institute, College of Art) and the Avery Graduate School (Bard College). Author of over thirty books of poetry, fiction, and criticism. Directs Black Square Editions, a not-for-profit press. Collaborations with artists (Norman Bluhm, Max Gimblett, Edward Henderson, Bill Jensen, Bodo Korsig, Suzanne McClelland, Martin Noel, Jurgen Partenheimer, Archie Rand, Peter Saul, Hanns Schimansky, Pat Steir, Robert Therrien, and Dan Walsh) include one-of-a-kind works, multiples, and books. Grants and fellowships from the NEA, NYFA (twice), and the Ingram Merrill Foundation (twice), and has been awarded a General Electric Foundation Award, a Lavan Award (Academy of American Poets), and the Brendan Gill Award. Lives with the artist Eve Aschheim and their daughter Cerise Tzara in Manhattan.